THE
POWER
OF *I AM*
Journal

Also by Joel Osteen

Break Out!
Break Out! Journal
Daily Readings from Break Out!
Every Day a Friday
Every Day a Friday Journal
Daily Readings from Every Day a Friday
Fresh Start
Fresh Start Study Guide
I Declare
I Declare Personal Application Guide
The Power of I AM
The Power of I AM Study Guide
You Can, You Will
You Can, You Will Journal
Daily Readings from You Can, You Will
Your Best Life Now
Daily Readings from Your Best Life Now
Your Best Life Begins Each Morning
Your Best Life Now Study Guide
Your Best Life Now for Moms
Your Best Life Now Journal
Starting Your Best Life Now

THE
POWER
OF *I AM*
Journal

Two Words That Will
Change Your Life Today

JOEL OSTEEN
#1 *New York Times* Bestselling Author

FaithWords

New York • Boston • Nashville

Literary development: Koechel Peterson & Associates, Inc., Minneapolis, Minnesota.

This book has been adapted from *The Power of I Am* © 2015 by Joel Osteen. Published by FaithWords.

FaithWords
Hachette Book Group
1290 Avenue of the Americas
New York, NY 10104

www.faithwords.com

Printed in the United States of America

First Edition: March 2016

10 9 8 7 6 5 4 3 2 1

FaithWords is a division of Hachette Book Group, Inc. The FaithWords name and logo are trademarks of Hachette Book Group, Inc.

The Hachette Speakers Bureau provides a wide range of authors for speaking events. To find out more, go to www.hachettespeakersbureau.com or call (866) 376-6591.

The publisher is not responsible for websites (or their content) that are not owned by the publisher.

ISBN: 978-1-6094-1899-1

contents

introduction

D o you long to discover unique abilities and advantages you never knew you had that can lead to a more productive and happier life? Do you want to build the quiet confidence to face any obstacle that comes your way? Have you wondered if you have inner strengths, natural talents, and unique abilities that will make you prosper with self-assurance and success?

That is why I wrote my bestselling book *The Power of I AM*. In it I reveal a simple yet profound principle that can help you attain these dreams and goals. With the words "I am," you can control your success or failure, transform your self-image, invite the right things into your life, and redirect your life's course onto the road of your destiny.

I AM. Can these two words give you the power to change your life? Yes they can! Why? Because what follows these two words will determine the course of your life. Whatever follows the words "I am" will always come looking for you. So when you go through the day saying, "I am blessed," blessings pursue you. When you say, "I am healthy," health heads your way. When you say, "I am strong," strength tracks you down. That is life-changing!

This journal companion offers a practical tool that will help you harness *The Power of I AM* and become who God made you to be—an amazing, original masterpiece chosen by the Most High God to do great things. It offers the same encouragement in daily doses supplemented by inspirational and thought-provoking material. You will find a wealth of scriptures, inspirational quotations, selected stories, prayers, and points for contemplation. All are provided to engage you in a process of reflection that will enhance your faith and help you to rise to a new level of being your best.

I am delighted in your interest in this journal. It shows that you want to put your faith into action and reach the highest level of your destiny, and God loves that. You'll learn nineteen powerful "I am"s for your life that will help take you there. It's time to stop criticizing yourself and discover an extraordinary life.

This journal is an open door to self-discovery, so step through and begin the journey toward living the life you were born to live. My prayer is that you will take some time each day to read the entries and to add your own thoughts. But don't rush through it. Slow yourself down and take the time to reflect on your life. Let the scriptures speak to your heart. If you are facing challenges or barriers, there are prayers and inspirational quotes to help remind you that God is with you each and every moment. Be still and listen to what God is saying through these words, then put words to your responses.

This is a journal to record life lessons that you don't want to forget. It could be the start to a brand-new beginning for you. Underline important ideas within these pages, write yourself notes of encouragement in the margins as you read, and jot down fresh ideas that come to you as you read. Especially seek God's help and guidance regarding areas in which He may want to change you. It's a reflection of your life journey. What you record you remember. You will discover that it will bring clarity to what God has done, is doing, and wants to do in your life.

Journaling has also been shown to improve problem-solving abilities. Many people find that using a journal helps them to better assess their thoughts and feelings and to find clarity. The process of putting pen to paper and then seeing your words on the page can help you solve problems while keeping matters in perspective and priorities straight. You may release pent-up emotions in the process, and that is a good thing too.

Be as honest as possible as you write your responses. Don't be afraid to freely express your thoughts and feelings. Don't worry about punctuation, spelling, or grammar when making your own entries. You won't be graded on this.

This journal is designed to provide you nineteen days of daily inspiration and encouragement in your walk of faith. It is best to read day to day in a quiet place where you can meditate and contemplate for brief periods, away from the usual distractions. Take your time and enter your thoughts and encouragements. Once you've gone through it, feel free to begin again. Replenish your spirit and listen for the still, small voice of God's grace and direction.

Let this journal serve as a record of your daily progress and your entries as a testimony of your faith. Enjoy the process. You may have had some victories in the past, but you haven't seen anything yet.

No matter what challenges or troubles you face, you can choose to rise to a new level and invite God's goodness into your life by focusing on these two words, I AM!

FORGIVEN BLESSED

QUALIFIED

PROSPEROUS

CONFIDENT

MOTIVATED

TALENTED PROSPEROUS

BLESSED

STRONG

THE
POWER
of "I AM"

CHAPTER ONE

Key Truth

What follows the two simple words "I am" will determine what kind of life you live. The "I am"s that are coming out of your mouth will bring either success or failure, because whatever follows the "I am" will always come looking for you.

THE
POWER
of "I AM"

Few of us are aware of it, but all through the day, there is a powerful dynamic playing out in our life that brings us success or failure. It is not about our family background, education, personality, intellect, or skills. Rather, it starts in the beliefs we have about ourselves that are then declared through the "I am"s that come out of our mouths. You know, when you're putting on your clothes and whisper, "I am so overweight," or you see somebody whom you think is more talented and say, "I am so average."

So what's so dynamic and powerful about something we do all the time? Well, here's the principle: *Whatever follows the "I am" will always come looking for you.* When you say, "I never get good breaks," disappointment is on the way. When you go through the day saying, "I am blessed," blessings come looking for you. Whatever you follow the "I am" with, you're handing it an invitation, opening the door, and giving it permission to be in your life. That is a phenomenal power that we wield for or against ourselves!

What kind of "I am"s are coming out of your mouth? "I am victorious. I am talented. I am anointed." When you have the right "I am"s, you're inviting the goodness of God. Maybe if you would just change the "I am," you would rise to a new level. Words have creative power. Proverbs 18:21 says, "Life and death are in the power of our tongue." It's up to you to choose what follows the "I am"s in your life. My encouragement is to never say negative things about yourself. That is cursing your future. Do yourself a favor and zip that up. Don't be against yourself.

Romans 4 says to "call the things that are not as though they were." That simply means that you shouldn't talk about the way you are. Talk about the way you want to be. If you're struggling in your finances, don't go around saying, "Oh, man, I'm never going to pay off my debt." That's calling the things that are as if they will always be that way. That's just describing the situation. By faith you have to say, "I am blessed. I am successful. I am surrounded by God's favor."

Have you allowed what somebody—a coach, a teacher, a parent, an ex-spouse—said about you to hold you back? They've planted negative seeds of what you cannot do. "You're not smart enough. You're not talented enough. You're not attractive enough. You'll always be mediocre. You'll always struggle with your weight." Get rid of those lies! That is not who you are. You are who God says you are.

When God made you, He stepped back and said, "I like that. That was good. Another masterpiece!" He stamped His approval on you. Other people may try to disapprove you. Don't go around feeling less than, feeling inferior. Our attitude should be: *I am approved by Almighty God. I am accepted. I am a masterpiece.* When you talk like that, the seeds of greatness God has placed on the inside will begin to spring forth.

Consider This

David said in Psalm 139, "God, I praise You because You have made me in an amazing way. What You have done is wonderful." He was saying, not in pride but in praise to God, "I am wonderful. I am amazing. I am a masterpiece." That is just as true for you, because you were created in the image of Almighty God. Be bold and take David's declaration and write out your own, starting with your name.

....
....
....
....
....
....
....
....
....
....
....
....
....
....
....
....
....
....
....
....

What the Scriptures Say

By the grace of God I am what I am,
and His grace toward me was not in vain.

1 Corinthians 15:10

Surely, LORD, you bless the righteous;
you surround them with your favor as with a shield.

Psalm 5:12

I thank you Father for surrounding me with your favor & that I listen to your voice & follow your leading in every day that I live. Thank you for surrounding me with your shield of protection every where I live & work & play. Thank you for defending me in any conflict or situation. Thank you for all the friends you have given me.

Thoughts for Today

The only place where your dream becomes
impossible is in your own thinking.

Robert H. Schuller

The greatest discovery of my generation is that human beings
can alter their lives by altering their attitudes of mind.

William James

There are no constraints on the human mind,
no walls around the human spirit, no barriers to
our progress except those we ourselves erect.

Ronald Reagan

. . . .
. . . .
. . . .
. . . .
. . . .
. . . .
. . . .
. . . .
. . . .
. . . .
. . . .
. . . .
. . . .
. . . .

A Prayer for Today

Father, Your Word says that I can call the things that are not as though they were. Thank You that my words have creative power and that I can use my words to become who I want to be. Thank You that I am not limited by what people have spoken negatively over my life, but I am who You say I am. I praise You that You call me a master-piece. I believe that You have created me in Your image and that the seeds of greatness You have placed inside of me are springing to life.

takeaway
TRUTH

You need to send out some new invitations. Get up in the morning and invite good things into your life. "I am blessed. I am strong. I am talented. I am wise. I am disciplined. I am focused. I am prosperous." When you talk like that, talent gets summoned by Almighty God: "Go find that person." Health, strength, abundance, and discipline start heading your way.

SECURE

HEALTHY

POSITIVE

PROSPEROUS

MOTIVATED

PROSPEROUS

CREATIVE

CONFIDENT

BLESSED

TALENTED

QUALIFY

BE
POSITIVE
or *BE QUIET*

CHAPTER TWO

Key Truth

You are where you are today in part because of what you've been saying about yourself. Words are like seeds. When you speak something out, you give life to what you're saying. If you continue to say it, eventually that can become a reality.

THE
POWER
of "I AM"

The Scripture says, "We will eat the fruit of our words." When you talk, you are planting seeds. At some point, you're going to reap fruit from the exact seeds that you've been sowing. Whether you realize it or not, you are prophesying your future.

This is great when we're saying things such as, "I'm blessed. I will accomplish my dreams. I'm coming out of debt." That's not just being positive; you are actually prophesying victory, prophesying success, prophesying new levels. Your life will move in the direction of your words. But too many people go around prophesying just the opposite. "I never get any breaks. I'll never get back in shape. I'll probably get laid off. I always get the flu." They don't realize they are prophesying defeat.

Proverbs 6 states, "We are snared by the words of our mouth." *Snared* means "to be trapped." What you say can keep you from your potential and set limits for your life. You're not snared by what you think. Negative thoughts come to us all. But when you speak them out, you give them life. That's when they become a reality. When you say, "I never get any good breaks," that stops the favor that was ordained to you. If you say, "I'm not that talented. I don't have a good personality," that is calling in mediocrity. When negative thoughts come, the key is to never verbalize them. That thought will die stillborn if you don't speak it.

God gave Jeremiah a promise that he would become a great prophet to the nations (Jeremiah 1). But when he heard God's voice, he was very young and unsure of himself. He instead listened to the other voice of doubt and defeat and said, "God, I can't do that. I'm too young. I wouldn't know what to say." God said, "Jeremiah, say not that you are too young."

The first thing God did was to stop his negative words. Why did God do that? Because He knew that if Jeremiah went around saying, "I'm not qualified. I can't do this. I don't have what it takes," he would become exactly what he was saying. So God said in effect, "Jeremiah, zip it up. You may think it, but don't speak it out." It goes on to tell how Jeremiah changed what he was saying, and he became a prophet to the nations.

When God told Joshua and the people of Israel to march around the walled city of Jericho for seven straight days, He said, "While you march, don't say one word, not a whisper. Keep totally silent." God knew that after a couple of times around the perimeter of the city, they would be saying, "What in the world are we doing out here? This wall is never going to fall." God knew they would talk themselves out of it. He was saying in effect, "I know you're not going to be positive, so just stay silent."

Don't let your negative words keep you from God's best. If you'll stop talking defeat, lack, how it's not going to happen, and simply remain silent, God can do for you what He did for them. He knows how to bring those walls down.

Consider This

In life, there are always two voices competing
for your attention—the voice of faith and the voice of
defeat. One voice will point out that you've reached your
limits. The other voice is clear and matter-of-fact: "You are
well able. You can do all things through Christ." Describe
what the voices say in your life. Write down the words
of faith that you will speak out loud to see God release
His promises for your life.

....
....
....
....
....
....
....
....
....
....
....
....
....
....
....
....
....

What the Scriptures Say

Set a guard, O LORD, over my mouth;
keep watch over the door of my lips.

Psalm 141:3

Then the word of the LORD came to me, saying:
"Before I formed you in the womb I knew you; before you
were born I sanctified you; I ordained you a prophet to the
nations." Then said I: "Ah, Lord GOD! Behold, I cannot speak,
for I am a youth." But the LORD said to me: "Do not say,
'I am a youth,' for you shall go to all to whom I send you, and
whatever I command you, you shall speak. Do not be afraid of
their faces, for I am with you to deliver you," says the LORD.
Then the LORD put forth His hand and touched my mouth,
and the LORD said to me: "Behold, I have put My
words in your mouth."

Jeremiah 1:4–9

....
....
....
....
....
....
....
....
....
....
....

Thoughts for Today

When you have spoken the word, it reigns over you.
When it is unspoken, you reign over it.

Ancient Proverb

Be careful of your thoughts,
they may become words at any moment.

Iara Gassen

Among my most prized possessions are words
that I have never spoken.

Orson Scott Card

....
....
....
....
....
....
....
....
....
....
....
....
....
....
....

A Prayer for Today

Father, thank You that I do not have to keep being snared by the words of my mouth. Thank You that You have given me the free choice to zip my lips when I have negative thoughts. Help me to not just stop speaking negative words that prophesy defeat, but help me use my words wisely to prophesy victory, success, and new levels for my life. I believe that as I speak words of faith out loud that I will see You release Your promises in my life.

takeaway *TRUTH*

Don't let your negative words stop what God wants to do. If you can't say anything positive, zip the lips. You may think it, but don't give it life by speaking it out. When you make this adjustment, God is going to release promises that have been delayed. Your healing, your vindication, and your promotion are right up in front of you.

MOTIVATED SECURE DISCIPLINED FORGIVEN PROSPEROUS CONFIDENT MOTIVATED TALENTED PROSPEROUS BLESSED STRONG

SAY SO

CHAPTER THREE

Key Truth

Words have creative power. When you speak something out, you give life to your faith. The Scripture says, "Let the redeemed of the LORD *say so.*" It doesn't say, "Let the redeemed think so, or believe so, or hope so." That's all good, but you have to take it one step further and *say so.*

THE
POWER
of "*I AM*"

Words have creative power. When God created the worlds, He didn't just think them into being. He didn't just believe there would be light and land and oceans and animals. He had it in His heart, but nothing happened until He spoke. He said, "Let there be light," and light came. His thoughts didn't set it into motion; His words set it into motion.

It's the same principle today. You can have faith in your heart, big dreams, be standing on God's promises, and never see anything change. What's the problem? Nothing happens until you speak. The Scripture says, "Let the redeemed of the Lord *say so*." It doesn't say, "Let the redeemed think so, or believe so, or hope so." When you speak, just like when God spoke, things begin to happen. Opportunities will find you. Good breaks, promotion, and ideas will track you down.

Psalm 91 says, "I will say of the Lord, 'He is my refuge, my fortress, and my shield.'" The next verse says, "He will deliver me, protect me, and cover me." Notice the connection. *I will say* and *He will do*. It doesn't say, "I believe He is my refuge. I believe He will be my strength." The psalmist went around declaring it, speaking it out: "The Lord is my refuge. The Lord is my strength." Notice what happened. God became his refuge and strength. God was saying in effect, "If you're bold enough to speak it, I'm bold enough to do it."

When David faced Goliath, it looked impossible. All the odds were against him. He could have easily said, "Look, he's a giant.

He's got more experience, more equipment, more talent. I can't fight him." Negative words can keep you from becoming who you were created to be. Instead, David looked Goliath in the eyes and said, "You come against me with a sword and a shield. But I come against you in the name of the Lord God of Israel. This day, I will defeat you!" Notice he was prophesying victory. He may have felt fear, but he spoke faith.

In the Old Testament, Ezekiel saw a vision of a valley filled with bones. It was like a huge graveyard of bones from people who had died. Bones represent things in our life that look dead, situations that seem impossible and permanently unchanging. God told him, "Ezekiel, prophesy to these dead bones. Say, 'Oh, you dry bones, hear the word of the Lord.'" As Ezekiel started speaking to the bones, telling them to come back to life, the bones started rattling and coming together, just like out of a movie, morphing back into a person. Finally, God told him to "prophesy to the breath" and call it forth. The Scripture says, "As he prophesied, breath came into those bodies, and they stood up like a vast army."

You may have things in your life that seem dead—a relationship, a business, your health. All you can see is a valley of dry bones, so to speak. Prophesy to those dead bones. Call in health. Call in abundance. Call in restoration. God will resurrect what looks dead. He'll make things happen that you could never make happen.

Consider This

Have you ever declared that your dreams are coming to pass? Have you ever said, "I will pay off my house"? "I will start my own business." "I will get my degree." "I will lose this weight." "I will see my family restored." What has God put in your heart that you need to *say so* and see your faith be released?

....
....
....
....
....
....
....
....
....
....
....
....
....
....
....
....
....
....
....
....

What the Scriptures Say

Let the redeemed of the LORD say so, whom
He has redeemed from the hand of the enemy.

Psalm 107:2

Then he said to me, "Speak a prophetic message to
these bones and say, 'Dry bones, listen to the word of the
LORD! This is what the Sovereign LORD says: Look! I am going
to put breath into you and make you live again! I will put flesh
and muscles on you and cover you with skin. I will put breath
into you, and you will come to life. Then you will know
that I am the LORD.'"

Ezekiel 37:4–6

....
....
....
....
....
....
....
....
....
....
....
....
....
....

Thoughts for Today

The words that come out of our mouths go into our
own ears as well as other people's, and then they drop down
into our soul, where they give us either joy or sadness, peace or
upset, depending on the types of words we have spoken.

Joyce Meyer

Faith, mighty faith, the promise sees, and looks to God alone;
laughs at impossibilities, and cries it shall be done.

Charles Wesley

Freedom lies in being bold.

Carl Frost

....
....
....
....
....
....
....
....
....
....
....
....
....
....

A Prayer for Today

Father in heaven, thank You that when You created the
worlds, You didn't just think or believe them into being;
You spoke them into being. Your Word also declares I
am made in Your image, and I too should speak words
of faith over my life. Thank You that I can even speak to
the things in my life that seem dead, as Ezekiel did to the
valley of dry bones, and You will breathe life into them
and bring resurrection. I believe that as
I speak words of faith that You will make things
happen that I could never make happen.

takeaway
TRUTH

One of the best things you can do is take a few minutes every morning and make positive declarations over your life. Write down not only your dreams, your goals, and your vision, but make a list of any area you want to improve in, anything you want to see changed. Declare every day, "I am confident. I am valuable. I am one of a kind. I am a child of the Most High God," and you'll go out with your head held high.

FORGIVEN SECURE DISCIPLINED CONFIDENT PROSPEROUS MOTIVATED TALENTED PROSPEROUS BLESSED STRONG

I am Blessed:
A Magnet for
BLESSINGS

CHAPTER FOUR

Key Truth

When you honor God with your life,
keeping Him in first place, He puts something on
you called *a commanded blessing*, which is like
a magnet that attracts the right people, good
breaks, contracts, ideas, resources, and influence.
You become a magnet for God's goodness.

THE
POWER
of "*I AM*"

It says in Deuteronomy 28: "When you walk in God's ways, making pleasing Him your highest priority, all these blessings will chase you down and overtake you." One translation says, "You will become a magnet for blessings." You don't have to go after the right people, good breaks, contracts, ideas, resources, and influence, trying to make something happen in your own strength or talent. All you have to do is keep honoring God and the right people and opportunities will find you. The favor, the wisdom, and the vindication will track you down. Why? You've become a magnet for God's goodness.

When I look back over my life, it is evident that most of the favor and good breaks came to me. I didn't go after them. I was simply being my best, and God did more than I could ask or think. I spent seventeen years behind the scenes at Lakewood doing the television production. I'm not bragging, but during those seventeen years, I was faithful. I gave it my all. I wanted that broadcast to be perfect. I wasn't looking to become Lakewood's senior pastor. I was content where I was behind the scenes. But when my father went to be with the Lord, this opportunity came looking for me. I never planned on doing it; it chased me down.

What God has planned for you is much bigger than anything you've ever dreamed. If God were to show you right now where He's taking you—the favor, the promotion, the influence—it would boggle your mind. You may not be the most qualified or talented. That's okay. God's anointing on you is more important than your talent, your education, or what family you come from.

You may not see how this can happen. It doesn't seem possible. But you don't have to figure it out. If you'll just keep being your best right where you are, getting to work on time, doing more than you have to, being a person of excellence and integrity, the right people will find you and the right opportunities will track you down.

Here's the whole key. You don't have to seek the blessing. Seek God, and the blessings will seek after you. Proverbs 13 says, "The wealth of the ungodly will eventually find its way into the hands of the righteous for whom it has been laid up." Notice, because you're the righteous, there's something God has laid up for you. Keep honoring God, and He promises some of these "eventually"s will track you down.

Dream big. Believe big. Pray big. Make room for God to do something new in your life. God knows what He's put in you—the gifts, the talents, the potential. You have seeds of greatness on the inside. Doors are going to open that no man can shut. Talent is going to come out of you that you didn't know you had. God is going to connect you with the right people. He will present you with opportunities that will thrust you into a new level of your destiny. Proverbs says it this way: "Trouble chases sinners, while blessings chase the righteous!"

Consider This

Jesus said, "Seek first the kingdom and all these things will be added unto you." What is required for you to become a magnet for God's goodness? Is anything holding you back?

. . . .
. . . .
. . . .
. . . .
. . . .
. . . .
. . . .
. . . .
. . . .
. . . .
. . . .
. . . .
. . . .
. . . .
. . . .
. . . .
. . . .
. . . .
. . . .
. . . .
. . . .
. . . .

What the Scriptures Say

"I will give you hidden treasures, riches stored
in secret places, so that you may know that I am the LORD,
the God of Israel, who summons you by name."

Isaiah 45:3

Jabez cried out to the God of Israel, "Oh, that you
would bless me and enlarge my territory! Let your hand
be with me, and keep me from harm so that I will be
free from pain." And God granted his request.

1 Chronicles 4:10

Thoughts for Today

Have you ever thought that in every action
of grace in your heart you have the whole omnipotence
of God engaged to bless you?

Andrew Murray

However many blessings we expect from God, His infinite liberality will always exceed all our wishes and our thoughts.

John Calvin

God has great things in store for His people;
they ought to have large expectations.

C. H. Spurgeon

....

....

....

....

....

....

....

....

....

....

....

....

....

....

A Prayer for Today

Father in heaven, thank You for the promise
that if I make pleasing You my highest priority and
I walk in Your ways, You have an abundance of blessings
that will chase me down and overtake me. Thank You that
I don't have to live my life trying to make things happen
on my own, but if I honor You, You will cause the right
things to find me. I believe that as I seek You and Your
kingdom first that doors of opportunity are going
to open that no man can shut and that You will
thrust me to a new level of my destiny.

takeaway
TRUTH

When you realize God has put a commanded blessing on your life, and you go out each day with the attitude that something good is going to happen to you, that's when God can do the exceedingly, abundantly, above and beyond. He has explosive blessings coming your way. They are going to thrust you to a level greater than you've imagined. All through the day, make this declaration: "I am blessed."

SECURE
DISCIPLINED
CONFIDENT
FORGIVEN
PROSPEROUS
MOTIVATED
TALENTED PROSPEROUS
STRONG
BLESSED

I am FREE:
Your Seventh
YEAR

CHAPTER FIVE

Key Truth

God gave the people of Israel a law that said every seventh year they had to release any Hebrew slaves. If you were a part of God's chosen people, no matter how much you still owed on a debt that had enslaved you, you were set free. You are coming into your seventh year. God is releasing you into opportunity, into favor, into healing, and into breakthroughs.

THE
POWER
of "*I AM*"

When we've struggled in an area for a long time, it's easy to think, *This is the way it's always going to be.* Too often we see it as permanent. People tell me, "I've always been negative. That's just who I am." They've convinced themselves that it's never going to change.

The first place we lose the battle is in our own thinking. If you think it's permanent, then it's permanent. If you think you've reached your limits, you have. If you think you'll never get well, you won't. You have to change your thinking. You need to see everything that's holding you back as only temporary. It didn't come to stay; it came to pass. The moment you accept it as the norm, it can take root and become a reality. A stronghold in your mind can keep you from your destiny. If you would just break out in your thinking, you would see things begin to improve.

In Deuteronomy 15, there was a law God gave the people of Israel that said every seventh year they had to release any Hebrew slaves. If you were Hebrew and owed someone money that you couldn't pay, they could enslave you and make you work until you paid them back. But every seventh year, if you were one of God's chosen people, no matter how much you still owed, you were set free.

God never intended His people to be permanent slaves to anything. The seventh year is when you break free from any limitation that is holding you back—sickness, addictions, debt, constant struggles. You are a child of the Most High God. You have an advantage. God promised you're not going to be a permanent slave to anything.

In the Scripture, King Hezekiah was very sick and had been told by the prophet Isaiah that he was going to die. It looked permanent, as though his days were over. Hezekiah could have accepted it and thought, *It's my lot in life.* But Hezekiah had a boldness. He chose to believe even when it looked impossible. The Scripture says, "He turned his face to the wall and started praying." Before Isaiah could leave the palace grounds, God spoke to him and said, "Go back and tell Hezekiah that I'm going to give him fifteen more years." Here's what I want you to see. Hezekiah's faith brought about his seventh year. Faith is what causes God to move.

God is saying, "Get ready. You are coming into your seventh year." You have to receive this into your spirit today. The seventh year is a year of release from sickness, disease, and chronic pain. Release from depression, worry, bad habits, and addictions. It's not only a release from limitations; it's a release into increase. God is about to release you into new opportunities, good breaks, and new levels. He is going to release ideas, creativity, sales, contracts, and business. The seventh year is when you get released into overflow, into more than enough. It's when dreams come to pass because things have shifted in your favor.

Consider This

Isaiah said, "The Spirit of the Lord is upon me to announce freedom to the captives." Then he took it one step further. "I'm declaring the Year of God's Favor." He announced it, then he declared it. What areas of your life do you need to announce that you're coming out of and declare you're coming into increase, overflow, and abundance?

....
....
....
....
....
....
....
....
....
....
....
....
....
....
....
....
....
....
....

What the Scriptures Say

Then the LORD said: "I am making a covenant with you.
Before all your people I will do wonders never before done in
any nation in all the world. The people you live among will see
how awesome is the work that I, the LORD, will do for you."

Exodus 34:10

"At the end of every seven years you shall grant
a release of debts. And this is the form of the release: Every
creditor who has lent anything to his neighbor shall release it;
he shall not require it of his neighbor or his brother,
because it is called the LORD's release."

Deuteronomy 15:1–2

Thoughts for Today

Sorrow looks back. Worry looks around. Faith looks ahead.

Beatrice Fallon

He brought light out of darkness, not out of a lesser light, and He can bring your summer out of winter, though you have no spring. Though in the ways of fortune, understanding, or conscience you have been benighted until now, wintered and frozen, clouded and eclipsed, damped and benumbed, smothered and stupefied, now God comes to you, not as the dawning of the day, not as the bud of the spring, but as the sun at noon.

John Donne

The divine art of miracle is not an art of suspending the pattern to which events conform, but of feeding new events into that pattern.

C. S. Lewis

....
....
....
....
....
....
....
....
....
....
....

A Prayer for Today

Father God, thank You for the promise that
I am coming into my seventh year, that You are bringing
me freedom and breaking the yokes of any limitation that
has held me back. Thank You that this is the year of Your
favor when strongholds are shattered that are trying to
keep me from my destiny. I believe and declare that I am
free in Christ and coming into breakthroughs, increase,
healings, overflow, and abundance.

....
....
....
....
....
....
....
....
....
....
....
....
....
....
....
....
....
....
....
....

takeaway
TRUTH

This is a new day. Every chain has been loosed. Every stronghold has been shattered. You are breaking free into a new level. You have to change what's coming out of your mouth. Dare to start boldly declaring, "I am free. I am healthy. I am blessed. I am victorious. God's favor is coming—breakthroughs, healing, and promotions are on the way."

SECURE
DISCIPLINED
FORGIVEN
PROSPEROUS
QUALIFIED APPROVED
CONFIDENT
MOTIVATED
TALENTED PROSPEROUS

I am VALUABLE:
Know Who
YOU ARE

CHAPTER SIX

Key Truth

When God created you in His image, He put a part
of Himself in you. He is not just the Creator of the
universe. He is your Heavenly Father. You have
His DNA. Imagine what you can do.

THE POWER of "*I AM*"

When God created you in His image, He put a part of Himself in you. You could say that you have the DNA of Almighty God. You are destined to do great things, destined to leave your mark on this generation. Your Heavenly Father spoke worlds into existence. He flung stars into space. He designed every flower. He made man out of dust and breathed life into him. Now here's the key. He is not just the all-powerful God. He is your Heavenly Father. You have His DNA. Imagine what you can do.

But too many times we focus on our weaknesses and mistakes, what we don't have, and the family we come from. We end up settling for mediocrity when we were created for greatness. If you're going to break out of average, you need to remind yourself of who you are because of who your Father is.

When you gave your life to Christ, the Scripture talks about how you became a new creation. You were born into a new family. You entered into a new royal bloodline. You are God's child. You have His spiritual DNA. So don't you dare go around thinking that you're average. Your Father created worlds. There's nothing too much for you. You can overcome that sickness. You can run that company. You can take your family to a new level. Quit believing the lies that say, "You've reached your limits." Start talking to yourself as a winner. It's in your blood.

If you look back and study your spiritual bloodline in the family of God, you'll see your ancestor Moses parted the Red

Sea. There's great faith in your bloodline. David, a shepherd boy, defeated a giant. There's favor in your bloodline. Nehemiah rebuilt the walls of Jerusalem when all the odds were against him. There's increase, promotion, and abundance in your bloodline. A young lady named Esther stepped up and saved her people from a certain death. There is courage in your bloodline. When thoughts tell you that it's never going to happen, just check your spiritual birth certificate. Remind yourself of who you are.

In Judges 6, an angel appeared to a man named Gideon, who was hiding in the fields after a powerful nation had overtaken the people of Israel, and said, "Mighty hero, the Lord is with you." Gideon felt that he was just the opposite—he was the least, inadequate, and not able to deliver his people. It seemed that he was just another ordinary, insignificant man. But God saw something in Gideon that other people did not see. God saw his potential. God saw what he could become.

Gideon didn't know who he was, and the same is often true for us. You may feel that you're average. You may think you're ordinary, but God sees the mighty hero in you. God sees the DNA of a champion. He sees the king's son, the king's daughter. Now do yourself a favor. Turn off the negative recording that's reminding you of what you're not, and get in agreement with God. Start seeing yourself as that mighty hero.

Consider This

When God told Moses to go speak to Pharaoh and tell him to let the people go, the first thing Moses said was, "Who am I?" He was saying, "God, I'm ordinary. He is not going to listen to me." Moses forgot who he was. What areas of your life do you need to remind yourself of who you are?

....
....
....
....
....
....
....
....
....
....
....
....
....
....
....
....
....
....
....
....
....
....

What the Scriptures Say

The angel of the LORD came and sat down under the oak in Ophrah that belonged to Joash the Abiezrite, where his son Gideon was threshing wheat in a winepress to keep it from the Midianites. When the angel of the LORD appeared to Gideon, he said, "The LORD is with you, mighty warrior."

Judges 6:11–12 NIV

For if, by the trespass of the one man, death reigned through that one man, how much more will those who receive God's abundant provision of grace and of the gift of righteousness reign in life through the one man, Jesus Christ!

Romans 5:17

Thoughts for Today

Don't assume you have to be extraordinary to be used by God. You don't have to have exceptional gifts, talents, abilities, or connections. God specializes in using ordinary people whose limitations and weaknesses make them ideal showcases for His greatness and glory.

Nancy Leigh DeMoss

"Father" is the most significant name of the God of the Bible. It is the name that sets Christianity apart from all the other religions of the world, inviting us to believe in a Son and to enter into an intimate family relationship with a loving Father. Jesus, the Son of God, came so that we could meet His Father, be adopted into the family of God, and relate to the Almighty God of the universe in an intimate, personal, concrete way as sons and daughters.

Mary Kassian

The God who made us also can remake us.

Woodrow Kroll

....
....
....
....
....
....
....
....

A Prayer for Today

Father God, thank You that You created me in Your image and have made me Your child. Thank You that because You are my Father, I have a destiny to do great things. Thank You that I don't have to settle for mediocrity or to ever say I've reached my limit. I am Your child and I have a royal bloodline. I believe that I am going to soar to new heights and become everything You have created me to be.

takeaway
TRUTH

Friend, you come from a bloodline of champions. Get up every morning and check your spiritual birth certificate. Remind yourself of who you are. If you do this, I believe and declare, you're going to soar to new heights. You're going to rise above every obstacle. You're going to set new levels for your family and become everything God has created you to be.

FORGIVEN SECURE DISCIPLINED CONFIDENT PROSPEROUS MOTIVATED TALENTED QUALIFIED APPROVED PROSPEROUS BLESSED STRONG

I am a Masterpiece:
See Yourself as a
MASTERPIECE

CHAPTER SEVEN

Key Truth

When God created you, He went to great
lengths to make you exactly as He wanted.
If you're going to reach your highest potential,
you have to see yourself as unique, as an original,
as God's very own masterpiece.

THE POWER of "I AM"

Ephesians 2:10 says, "We are God's masterpiece." When God created you, He designed you on purpose to be the way you are. You didn't accidentally get your personality, your height, your looks, your skin color, or your gifts. There will never be another you. You have what you need to fulfill your destiny. If you're going to reach your highest potential, you have to see yourself as unique, as an original, as God's very own masterpiece.

You are God's most prized possession. Our value doesn't come because of what we look like, or what we do, or who we know. Our value comes from the fact that Almighty God is our Painter. When God created you, He stepped back and looked and said, "You're amazing. You're wonderful. Another masterpiece!" He stamped His approval on you. So don't criticize what God has painted. Quit wishing you were taller, or had a different personality, or looked like somebody else. You have been fearfully and wonderfully made. Accept yourself. Approve yourself. Get in agreement with what God says about you.

Jesus said to love your neighbor as you love yourself. If you don't love yourself in a healthy way, you will never be able to love others in the way that you should. This is why some people don't have good relationships. If you don't get along with yourself, you'll never get along with others. We all have weaknesses, shortcomings, things that we wish were different. But God never designed us to go through life being against our self. The opinion you have of yourself is the most important opinion that you have. If you see yourself as less than, not talented, not valuable, you will convey those feelings, and people will treat you inferior. If you are proud of who God made you to be, people will see you as strong, talented, and valuable and treat you accordingly.

The Scripture talks about how God has made us to be kings and priests unto Him. Start carrying yourself as royalty. Not in arrogance, thinking that you're better than others, but in humility be proud of who God made you to be. You are not better than anyone else, but you are not less than anyone else. Understand, your Father created the whole universe. When He breathed His life into you and sent you to planet earth, you didn't come as ordinary. You didn't come as average. You are crowned not by people but by Almighty God. Now start thinking as royalty, talking as royalty, dressing as royalty, walking as royalty, and acting as royalty.

When Jesus was being baptized by John in the Jordan River, He had not performed a single miracle or spoken to any great crowds. But God said, "This is My beloved Son in whom I am well pleased." His Father was pleased with Him because of who He was and not because of anything He had or had not done. You may not be perfect, but God is not basing your value on your performance. He's looking at whether you have a heart to please Him. Now quit being down on yourself. Quit living condemned and dare to believe God has already approved you.

Consider This

How do you see yourself right now in the light
of Ephesians 2:10? What are the things about yourself
that you don't feel good about . . . the things that you
put yourself down about? What can you do to be
more confident in who God made you to be?

....

....

....

....

....

....

....

....

....

....

....

....

....

....

....

....

....

....

....

....

....

What the Scriptures Say

For we are God's masterpiece. He has created us anew in Christ Jesus, so we can do the good things he planned for us long ago.

Ephesians 2:10 NLT

Woe to him who strives with his Maker! . . .
Shall the clay say to him who fashions it, What do you think you are making? or, Your work has no handles?

Isaiah 45:9 AMP

....
....
....
....
....
....
....
....
....
....
....
....
....
....
....
....
....
....

Thoughts for Today

I would rather be what God chose to make
me than the most glorious creature that I could think of;
for to have been thought about, born in God's thought,
and then made by God, is the dearest, grandest,
and most precious thing in all thinking.

George MacDonald

Dream lofty dreams, and as you dream, so shall you become.
Your vision is the promise of what you shall one day be.

James Allen

An infinite God can give all of Himself to each
of His children. He does not distribute Himself that
each may have a part, but to each one He gives all of
Himself as fully as if there were no others.

A. W. Tozer

A Prayer for Today

Father, thank You that I didn't accidentally get my personality, my looks, my gifts, my skin color, or my height. Thank You that I am Your masterpiece and I am fearfully and wonderfully made, and that's what You have declared about me. Help me to love myself, with all of my weaknesses and shortcomings and things that I wish were different. Today I celebrate who You have made me and I believe You have crowned me to be royalty.

takeaway
TRUTH

God breathed His life into you and says, "You are excellent in every way." Get up every morning and remind yourself that your value comes because of whose you are. Be bold enough to celebrate who God made you to be. Be proud of who you are. Dare to say as David declared, "I am amazing. I am talented. I am one of a kind. I am a masterpiece."

SECURE

DISCIPLINED

FORGIVEN

CONFIDENT

PROSPEROUS

MOTIVATED

TALENTED

PROSPEROUS

BLESSED

STRONG

I am Content:
Living CONTENT

Key Truth

It's good to have dreams and goals, but if we're unhappy, frustrated, and discontent while we're waiting for promises to come to pass, we're dishonoring God. The right attitude is, I have learned how to be content, whether I'm abased or abounding, whether I have plenty or whether I'm in need.

THE
POWER
of "*I AM*"

We should always be stretching our faith, believing for something bigger and pursuing our dreams and goals. But while we're waiting for things to change, waiting for promises to come to pass, we shouldn't be discontent where we are. When we're unhappy, frustrated, and discontent, we're dishonoring God. We're so focused on what we want that we're taking for granted what we have.

The Apostle Paul said, "I have learned how to be content, whether I'm abased or abounding, whether I have plenty or whether I'm in need." Notice he had to *learn* to be content. It doesn't happen automatically. It's a choice we have to make. Being content doesn't mean that we don't want change, give up on our dreams, or settle where we are. It means we're not frustrated. We know God is working behind the scenes, and at the right time He will get us to where we're supposed to be.

I've found some situations will not change until we change. As long as we're frustrated, stressed out, and discontent about our job or the kids or the size of our house, that's going to keep us where we are. God's plan for our life is not to just make us comfortable but to grow us up, to mature us, so He can release more of His favor. We may not like where we are, but we wouldn't be there unless God had a purpose for it. God is going to use it to do a work in us. When we're content, we're growing. We're developing character. Our faith is being strengthened. You could easily complain, but you say, "Lord, thank You for this." That's passing the test. Instead of trying to change the situation, let it change you.

David spent *years* in the lonely shepherd's fields taking care of his father's sheep . . . *after* he had been chosen to be the next king of Israel. The prophet Samuel had already anointed him. David could have thought, *God, this isn't right. I've got big dreams. You promised me great things. What am I doing stuck out here with a bunch of sheep?*

But David understood this principle. He didn't live stressed or frustrated. He knew that God was in control, so he just kept being his best, going to work with a good attitude, grateful for where he was. Because he was content in the shepherd's fields, he made it to the throne, to the palace. As Paul did, he learned to be content and passed that test.

You may be in a difficult season right now, raising a small child, taking care of an elderly loved one, or perhaps dealing with an illness. A mistake we make too often is that we think that when we reach a certain goal, then we'll be happy. "As soon as . . . , I'll enjoy my life." That's not reality. If you don't learn to be content where you are, you won't be content when your dreams come to pass. And because you're waiting for things to change, you're missing the beauty of this moment, the joy of today. Don't go through life always wanting something else. See the gift in what you have right now.

Consider This

Life is full of seasons. There has to be planting seasons,
watering seasons, and maintaining seasons. Without going
through that process, you're not going to come into a harvest
season. Describe the season you are in. What challenges has it
brought to you that are making you stronger and developing
your character? During this season, what has God given
you to be grateful for?

....
....
....
....
....
....
....
....
....
....
....
....
....
....
....
....
....
....
....
....

What the Scriptures Say

I have learned in whatever state I am, to be content:
I know how to be abased, and I know how to abound.
Everywhere and in all things I have learned both to be full
and to be hungry, both to abound and to suffer need.
I can do all things through Christ who strengthens me.

Philippians 4:11–13

Now godliness with contentment is great gain.
For we brought nothing into this world, and it is certain
we can carry nothing out. And having food and clothing,
with these we shall be content.

1 Timothy 6:6–8

Thoughts for Today

True contentment is the power of getting out
of any situation all that there is in it.

G. K. Chesterton

Do not spoil what you have by desiring what
you have not; remember that what you now have
was once among the things you only hoped for.

Epicurus

The remarkable thing is, we have a choice every day
regarding the attitude we will embrace for the day.

Chuck Swindoll

....
....
....
....
....
....
....
....
....
....
....
....
....

A Prayer for Today

Father in heaven, thank You that no matter what
my circumstances are that I don't have to live stressed
and frustrated and discontent. Thank You that You have
a purpose in where I am and what I am doing and that I
can find joy in today and the beauty of this moment in my
life. I believe that You have me in the palm of Your hand,
that You are directing my steps, and You will get me to
where I'm supposed to be when the time is right.

....
....
....
....
....
....
....
....
....
....
....
....
....
....
....
....
....
....
....

takeaway
TRUTH

God has you in the palm of His hand. He is directing your steps. He knows where you are, what you like, and what you don't like. Instead of living discontented, frustrated, always wishing you were somewhere else, embrace the place where you are. See the good. Be grateful for what you have. Remember that often there are adversities and blessings in a season. Don't focus on the adversities. You have the grace to enjoy the blessings.

DISCIPLINED
SECURE
CONFIDENT
MOTIVATED
PROSPEROUS
FORGIVEN
PROSPEROUS
MOTIVATED
TALENTED PROSPEROUS
BLESSED
STRONG

I am Secure:
Be Comfortable with
WHO YOU ARE

CHAPTER NINE

Key Truth

God has given you a specific assignment in life
and gifted you with exactly what you need for the
race that's been designed for you. You don't have
to outperform, out build, outdrive, outrace, or
outproduce anyone. It's not about anyone else. It's
about becoming who God made you to be.

THE
POWER
of "*I AM*"

There is an underlying pressure in our society to be number one. If we're not the best, the leader, the fastest, the most talented, the most beautiful, or the most successful, we're taught to not feel good about ourselves. We have to work harder. We have to run faster. We must stay ahead.

One of the best things I've ever learned is to be comfortable with who God made me to be. I believe God has given me a specific assignment in life and gifted me with exactly what I need for the race that's been designed for me. I don't have to outperform anyone to feel good about myself. I don't have to out build, outdrive, outrace, out minister, or outproduce anyone. It's not about anyone else. It's about becoming who God made me to be.

I'm all for having goals, stretching, and believing big. That's important. But you have to accept the gift that God has given you. You shouldn't feel less than if someone seems to have a more significant gift. God has given you a gift that's unique, something that will propel you into your destiny and cause you to leave your mark on this generation.

Here's the key. You don't have to have a great gift for God to use it in a great way. Do you know what gift put David on the throne? It wasn't his leadership skills, his dynamic personality, or his ability to write and play music. It was his gift to sling a rock. That seemingly insignificant gift enabled him to defeat Goliath and eventually put David on the throne. Never discount any gift that God has given you.

Too often we pursue titles and positions, thinking we'll feel good about ourselves when we have them. Titles are fine, but you don't need a title to do what God has called you to do. Don't wait for people to approve you, affirm you, or validate you. Use your gift, and the title will come.

When David went out to face Goliath, his title was shepherd. People told him he was not qualified, too small, and would get hurt. What David had, and what you have, may seem small. You may feel intimidated and unqualified. That's okay. It didn't stop David. If you'll use what you have, God will breathe on it. His anointing on that simple gift will cause you to step into the fullness of your destiny.

A lot of times we think, *If I had their talent and looks and career, I'd be happy.* But the truth is that if you traded places, you wouldn't be fulfilled, because their gifts, talents, skills, and personality have been uniquely designed for their assignment. You could try to do what they're doing, but the problem is the anointing on your life is for your gifts, for what you're called to do. If you just be the best that you can be with what you have, there will be a fulfillment, a satisfaction. God will open up doors. He will get you to where you're supposed to be. When you're comfortable with who you are, walking in your anointing, you enjoy life.

Consider This

Competing with others is a frustrating way to live. In what ways do you find yourself caught up in competing and comparing with others? What results do you get from trying to outperform and impress others? How can you break out of that and start running your own race?

....
....
....
....
....
....
....
....
....
....
....
....
....
....
....
....
....
....
....
....

What the Scriptures Say

Am I now trying to win the approval of human beings,
or of God? Or am I trying to please people? If I were still
trying to please people, I would not be a servant of Christ.

Galatians 1:10 NIV

The fear of human opinion disables;
trusting in God protects you from that.

Proverbs 29:25 MSG

Thoughts for Today

Next to faith this is the highest art—to be content
with the calling in which God has placed you.

Martin Luther

Happiness is living by inner purpose, not by outer pressures.
Happiness is a happening-with-God.

David Augsburger

Real contentment must come from within.
You and I cannot change or control the world around us,
but we can change and control the world within us.

Warren Wiersbe

. . . .
. . . .
. . . .
. . . .
. . . .
. . . .
. . . .
. . . .
. . . .
. . . .
. . . .
. . . .
. . . .

A Prayer for Today

Father, thank You that You have given me a specific
assignment in life and gifted me with exactly what I need
for the race that I've been designed to run. Thank You that
I don't have to outperform or outproduce anyone, because
my assignment and race is unique to me. Thank You that
I can just be the best that I can be with what I have, and
You will take care of the rest. I believe that as I walk in
Your anointing for me that my gifts and talents will come
out to the full and bring glory to Your name.

takeaway
TRUTH

Friend, your race is run by one person—you. Don't compare yourself. Celebrate yourself. If you learn to be comfortable with who you are, you'll not only enjoy your life more, but you will rise higher, your gifts and talents will come out to the full, and you will become everything that God has created you to be!

BLESSED
MOTIVATED
SECURE
DISCIPLINED
PROSPEROUS
QUALIFIED APPROVED
CONFIDENT
FORGIVEN
PROSPEROUS
MOTIVATED
TALENTED PROSPEROUS
STR

I am Victorious:
It's Under
YOUR FEET

CHAPTER TEN

Key Truth

The Word of God says that God has put all things—every sickness, every obstacle, and every temptation—under our feet. He is going to use it as a stepping-stone to take you higher. It's just a matter of time before you break through to a new level.

THE
POWER
of "I AM"

ow we see our difficulties very often will determine whether or not we get out of them. When things mount against us, it's easy to start thinking, *This is never going to work out. I'll just have to learn to live with it.* But 1 Corinthians 15 talks about how God has put all things under our feet. If you're going to live in victory, you have to see every sickness, every obstacle, and every temptation as being under your feet. It's no match for you. It's just a matter of time before you walk it out.

This is what David did. He faced all kinds of enemies. He said in Psalm 59, "I will look down in triumph on *all* of my enemies." Notice that David said "*all* of my enemies." So what am I going to do with difficulties—the financial debt, the addiction, the weight problem? Look down. Why? Because they're all under my feet.

God stated, "I have given you power to tread on all the power of the enemy." Think of that word *tread*. One translation says "to trample." You are not weak, defeated, or inferior. You are full of "can do" power. The same Spirit that raised Christ from the dead lives on the inside of you. Now start putting obstacles and difficulties under your feet.

The Scripture says, "The joy of the Lord is your strength." Joy is an emotion, and yet it creates strength. When you're in tough times, you have to shake off the worry, the self-pity, the disappointment. Get your joy back. Have the right perspective. That sickness, that obstacle—it's under your feet. It's not going to defeat you. It's going to promote you.

In 2 Samuel 22, it says, "You have armed me with strength for the battle. You have put my enemies under my feet." God knows every battle that you will ever face, including every temptation and every obstacle. He has not only put it under your feet, but He has armed you with strength for that battle. He has already equipped you. Quit telling yourself, "This is too much. I can't handle it." The greatest force in the universe is breathing in your direction. Tap into that power. Start declaring, "This is under my feet. God is in control. I am well able. I can do all things through Christ. I am strong in the Lord."

Psalm 110 says, "God will make your enemies your footstool." What do you do with a footstool? You put your feet up on it and rest. When we face difficulties, too often we take matters into our own hands. We think, *They did me wrong. I'm going to pay them back.* Or our medical report is not good, and we're so uptight we can't sleep at night. But if you want God to make your enemy your footstool, you have to be still and know that He is God. It takes faith to say, "God, I know You are fighting my battles. You promised it would work out for my good. So I'm going to keep my joy and stay in peace."

Consider This

What difficulty are you facing today that you need
to put your feet up and rest, so to speak, and let God
make into your footstool? What truths about God will
help you to stay in peace and keep your joy when you're
feeling upset, anxious, and panicked?

What the Scriptures Say

For He must reign till He has put all enemies under
His feet. The last enemy that will be destroyed *is* death.
For "He has put all things under His feet."

1 Corinthians 15:25–27

"Behold, I give unto you power to tread on serpents
and scorpions, and over all the power of the enemy:
and nothing shall by any means hurt you."

Luke 10:19 KJV

....
....
....
....
....
....
....
....
....
....
....
....
....
....
....
....
....

Thoughts for Today

Remember, the triumphant Christian does not
fight for victory; he celebrates a victory already won.
The victorious life is Christ's business, not yours.

Reginald Wallis

One on God's side is a majority.

Wendell Phillips

Satan's purpose is to take from you what God has given you.

John Osteen

....
....
....
....
....
....
....
....
....
....
....
....
....
....
....

A Prayer for Today

Father, thank You that Your Word declares that
You have put all things—every sickness, every obstacle,
and every temptation—under my feet. Thank You that I
don't have to just learn to live with it or put up with it.
Thank You that You have given me power to tread on all
the power of the enemy because Your Spirit lives inside
of me. I believe that I can look down in faith and see my
obstacles as being stepping-stones to take me higher.

takeaway
TRUTH

If you look down and imagine your obstacles as being under your feet, God will make your enemies your footstool. Instead of being a stumbling block, it will be a stepping-stone. Nothing will keep you from your destiny. You will overcome every obstacle, defeat every enemy, and become everything God has created you to be.

FORGIVEN SECURE DISCIPLINED CONFIDENT PROSPEROUS MOTIVATED TALENTED PROSPEROUS STRONG BLESSED

I am Prosperous:
Have an Abundant
MENTALITY

CHAPTER ELEVEN

Key Truth

God is called El Shaddai, the God of More Than Enough. Not the God of Barely Enough or the God of Just Help Me Make It Through. He's the God of Abundance.

THE
POWER
of *"I AM"*

God's dream for your life is that you would be blessed in such a way that you could be a blessing to others. David said, "My cup runs over." God is an overflow God. He is called El Shaddai, the God of More Than Enough. Not the God of Barely Enough or the God of Just Help Me Make It Through. He's the God of Abundance.

Psalm 35 says, "Let them say continually, 'Let the Lord be magnified who takes pleasure in the prosperity of His children.'" The people of God were supposed to go around constantly saying, "God takes pleasure in prospering me." It was to help them develop this abundant mentality. Your life is moving toward what you're constantly thinking about. If you're always thinking thoughts of lack, not enough, and struggle, you're moving toward the wrong things. All through the day, meditate on these thoughts: overflow, abundance, God takes pleasure in prospering you.

The Scripture says God will supply our needs "according to His riches." So often we look at our situations and think, *I'll never get ahead. I'll never get out.* But it's not according to what you have; it's according to what He has. The good news is God owns it all. One touch of God's favor can blast you out of Barely Enough and put you into More Than Enough. God has ways to increase you beyond your normal income and what's predictable. Quit telling yourself, "This is all I'll ever have." Let go of that and have an abundant mentality. "I'm not staying here. I am blessed and prosperous. I am headed to the land of More Than Enough."

Jesus told a parable about a prodigal son. This young man left home and blew all of his money, wasted his inheritance, and decided to return home. When his father saw him—the father represents God—he said to the staff, "Go kill the fatted calf. We're going to have a party." But the older brother got upset. He said, "Dad, I've been with you this whole time, and you've never even given me a skinny goat."

You can survive in the land of Barely Enough to make it through. You can endure in the land of Just Enough to pay the bills. But that is not God's best. Your Heavenly Father is saying, "I have a fatted calf for you. I have a place for you in the land of More Than Enough."

My prayer for you is found in Deuteronomy 1:11. It says, "May the Lord God of your fathers increase you a thousand times more than you are." Can you receive that into your spirit? A thousand times more favor. A thousand times more resources. A thousand times more income. Most of the time our thinking goes *TILT!* It's because we've been hanging out with that skinny goat too long. It's time to cut him loose. It's time to have a fatted calf mentality. I believe and declare you won't live in the land of Just Enough or the land of Barely Enough, but you're coming into the land of More Than Enough.

Consider This

In *The Message* translation, Deuteronomy 28 states, "God will lavish you with good things. He will throw open the doors of His sky vaults and rain down favor. You will always be the top dog and never the bottom dog." If you were to see yourself on the top, what would you look like? Write a statement of faith that gives God the permission to lavish you with good things.

....
....
....
....
....
....
....
....
....
....
....
....
....
....
....
....
....
....

What the Scriptures Say

I am the LORD your God, who brought you up out of Egypt;
open wide your mouth, and I will fill it.

Psalm 81:10

And my God shall supply all your need according
to His riches in glory by Christ Jesus.

Philippians 4:19

....
....
....
....
....
....
....
....
....
....
....
....
....
....
....
....
....
....
....

Thoughts for Today

Jesus Christ opens wide the doors of the treasure
house of God's promises, and bids us go in and take
with boldness the riches that are ours.

Corrie ten Boom

God is always trying to give good things to us,
but our hands are too full to receive them.

Augustine

God will either give you what you ask, or something far better.

Robert Murray McCheyne

....
....
....
....
....
....
....
....
....
....
....
....
....
....
....

A Prayer for Today

Father God, thank You that You are El Shaddai,
the God of More Than Enough and not the God of Barely
Enough or the God of Just Help Me Make It Through.
You are the God of Abundance. Thank You that I can get
rid of the skinny goat mentality and develop an abundant
mentality. I believe that You are going to bring me into a
life of overflow and abundance, because You take pleasure
in prospering me. I believe I am coming into the land
of More Than Enough.

....
....
....
....
....
....
....
....
....
....
....
....
....
....
....
....
....
....

takeaway *TRUTH*

Get up every morning and say, "Lord, I want to thank You that You are opening up Your sky vaults today, raining down favor, and lavishing me with good things. I am prosperous." If you'll have this abundant mentality, you'll come into the land of More Than Enough.

BLESSED
FORGIVEN
MOTIVATED
SECURE
DISCIPLINED
PROSPEROUS
CONFIDENT
PROSPEROUS
TALENTED
MOTIVATED
PROSPEROUS
BLESSED
STRONG

I am Focused:
REDEEM
the Time

CHAPTER TWELVE

Key Truth

God has given you a present. It's called "today." What are you going to do with it? The Scripture tells us to redeem the time. That means, don't waste it. Don't live this day unfocused, undisciplined, and unmotivated. We have a responsibility to use our time wisely.

THE
POWER
of "*I AM*"

Time is more valuable than money. You can make more money, but you can't make more time. The Scripture tells us to redeem the time and use it wisely. That means, don't waste it. Don't live this day unfocused, undisciplined, and unmotivated. This day and this life is a gift. Are you living it to the full? With purpose and passion? Pursuing your dreams? Or are you distracted? Indifferent? Just doing whatever comes along? Are you in a job you don't like? Hanging out with people who are pulling you down? That's not redeeming the time; that's wasting the time. You're either investing your life or you're wasting it.

Many people are talented and have great potential, but they're not disciplined with how they spend their time. Paul said in Ephesians, "Make the most of every opportunity. Don't be vague and thoughtless, but live purposefully and accurately." If you're going to reach your highest potential, you have to be an "on purpose" person. You know where you're going, are focused on a plan, organized, and taking action. You're not vague, distracted, waiting to see what happens.

On a regular basis, you need to reevaluate what you're doing. Refocus your life. Get rid of any distractions. Paul said, "I run with purpose in every step." When we understand the value of time and see each day as the gift that it is, it helps us to keep the right perspective. You don't waste your valuable time fighting battles that don't matter—the conflicts that are not between you and your God-given destiny. If somebody has a problem with you, as long as you're being your best, doing what God's put in your heart, with all due respect, that's their problem and not yours. It is not your responsibility to make them happy or win their approval.

It's not only important how we spend our time, but with whom we spend it. The only thing that's keeping some people from a new level of their destiny is wrong friendships. To redeem the time may mean you have to prune some relationships that are not adding value to your life. Don't hang around people who are not going anywhere, who have no goals or dreams. If you hang out with jealous, critical, unhappy people, you will end up jealous, critical, and unhappy. That's what it says in Proverbs: When you walk with wise men, you will become wise.

When Jesus was on the earth, He was very selective with His friendships. Everyone wanted to be close to Him. But He chose only twelve disciples with whom to spend most of His highly valuable time. Out of those twelve, three were his close friends: Peter, James, and John. One could be considered his best friend, John. He was described as the disciple whom Jesus loved. You have to be careful who you allow in your inner circle. You may have twenty people you call friends, but make sure the two or three you choose to be close to you believe in you, stick up for you, and are with you through thick or thin. Invest your time wisely.

Consider This

The Scripture talks about living well spent lives.
What specific steps will you take to improve your
use of time and move forward toward your goals and
becoming who God's created you to be?

....
....
....
....
....
....
....
....
....
....
....
....
....
....
....
....
....
....

What the Scriptures Say

. . . making the very most of your time [on earth, recognizing and taking advantage of each opportunity and using it with wisdom and diligence], because the days are [filled with] evil.

Ephesians 5:16 AMP

All athletes are disciplined in their training. They do it to win a prize that will fade away, but we do it for an eternal prize. So I run with purpose in every step. I am not just shadowboxing.

1 Corinthians 9:25–26 NLT

....

....

....

....

....

....

....

....

....

....

....

....

....

....

....

....

Thoughts for Today

He lives long that lives well; and time
misspent is not lived, but lost.

Thomas Fuller

To waste time is to squander a gift from God.

John Blanchard

Time in itself is really not the problem, but people who use it
are. People who excuse their failures by saying, "I don't have
time" really are admitting to mismanagement of time.

Ted Engstrom

....
....
....
....
....
....
....
....
....
....
....
....
....
....
....

A Prayer for Today

Father God, thank You that You are calling me to invest my time, to redeem the time, and to run my life with purpose and passion. Help me to reevaluate what I am doing, to refocus my life, and to get rid of anything that's distracting me from Your plan for my life. Help me to know if there are relationships that I need to prune and friendships that I need to be careful about. I believe that as I use my time wisely that You will help me to flourish and I will see Your favor in new ways.

takeaway
TRUTH

Make this decision that you're going to be an on-purpose person. Set your goals and be disciplined to stick with it. This day is a gift. Make sure you're investing your time and not wasting it. If you do this, the seeds of greatness on the inside of you are going to take root and begin to flourish. You're going to see God's favor in new ways.

FORGIVEN SECURE DISCIPLINED CONFIDENT PROSPEROUS MOTIVATED TALENTED PROSPEROUS PROSPEROUS QUALIFIED APPROVED BLESSED STRONG

I am Determined:
Finishing
GRACE

CHAPTER THIRTEEN

Key Truth

God is "the author and the finisher of our faith." He has not only given you the grace to start but the grace to finish. You have to shake off the discouragement to quit. Finishing grace is available, but you have to tap into it.

THE
POWER
of "*I AM*"

It doesn't take a lot of effort to start things—a diet, school, a family. Starting is easy. Finishing is what can be difficult. Anyone can have a dream, but it takes determination, perseverance, and a made-up mind to see it come to pass. The question is not, "Will you start?" but "Will you finish?" Too many people start off well, but along the way they have some setbacks, get discouraged, and quit.

But God is called "the author and the finisher of our faith." He has not only given you the grace to start but the grace to finish. When you are tempted to give up on a dream, a relationship, or a project, you have to shake it off. If you will keep moving forward in faith, honoring God, you will come into a strength that you didn't have before, a force pushing you forward. That's finishing grace. That's God breathing in your direction, helping you to become who He created you to be.

When you are moving forward and taking new ground with a dream, a project, or a relationship, the enemy will work overtime to try to keep you from finishing. Don't get discouraged when you have setbacks, people come against you, or a negative medical report. That's a sign that you're moving toward your finish line.

It says in Philippians, "God began a good work in you, and He will continue to perform it until it is complete." One translation says, "He will bring you to a flourishing finish"—not a defeated finish, where you barely make it and are beat up and broke. You are coming to a flourishing finish, a finish more rewarding than you ever imagined.

As a teenager, God gave Joseph a big dream that one day he would rule a nation. But when Joseph was seventeen, everything went wrong. His brothers betrayed him and sold him into slavery in Egypt, where he was put in prison for years for something he didn't do. It looked as if his dream was dead. He must have been depressed, angry, bitter, and upset. Nothing had turned out right. But Joseph understood this principle. He knew he had the grace not only to start but to finish what God put in his heart. So he stayed in faith. He kept doing the right thing when the wrong thing was happening. And one day his dream miraculously came to pass.

The closer you get to your destiny, the tougher the battles become. The Scripture says, "As your days are, so shall your strength be." This means your strength will always be equivalent to what you need. If you were to get a negative medical report, you're going to have the strength to deal with it. You're not going to fall apart. Your strength will always match what you're up against. The psalmist said, "God is a very present help in times of need." In the difficulties of life, if you will get quiet and turn off the negative voices, you will feel a peace that passes understanding. You find that there is finishing grace for every season.

Consider This

Describe a challenge you are facing at the
moment for which you are tempted to quit. Where
is the pressure coming from? How do you think God
wants you to respond to it? How will you tap
into the strength of finishing grace?

....
....
....
....
....
....
....
....
....
....
....
....
....
....
....
....
....
....

What the Scriptures Say

Therefore we also, since we are surrounded by so
great a cloud of witnesses, let us lay aside every weight,
and the sin which so easily ensnares us, and let us run with
endurance the race that is set before us, looking unto Jesus, the
author and finisher of our faith, who for the joy that was set
before Him endured the cross, despising the shame, and has
sat down at the right hand of the throne of God.

Hebrews 12:1–2

But none of these things move me; nor do I count
my life dear to myself, so that I may finish my race with joy,
and the ministry which I received from the Lord Jesus,
to testify to the gospel of the grace of God.

Acts 20:24

Thoughts for Today

Never give up, for that is just the place
and time that the tide will turn.

Harriet Beecher Stowe

If I had to select one quality, one personal characteristic
that I regard as being most highly correlated with success,
whatever the field, I would pick the trait of persistence.
Determination. The will to endure to the end, to get knocked
down seventy times and get up off the floor saying,
"Here comes number seventy-one!"

Richard DeVos

Most people give up just when they're about to achieve success.
They quit on the one-yard line. They give up at the last minute
of the game, one foot from a winning touchdown.

H. Ross Perot

. . . .

. . . .

. . . .

. . . .

. . . .

. . . .

. . . .

. . . .

. . . .

. . . .

. . . .

A Prayer for Today

Father God, thank You that Jesus is the author and finisher of our faith and that I can follow in His footsteps.
Thank You that You have given me not just the grace to
start my race but to finish it. Thank You that You will give
me the strength to move forward through every season of
my life. I believe that You began a good work in me, and
You will bring me to a flourishing finish.

takeaway *TRUTH*

The Scripture talks about how the race is not for the swift or for the strong, but for those who endure till the end. You don't have to finish first. You're not competing with anybody else. Just finish your course. Keep your fire burning. You weren't created to give up. You have to dig your heels in and say, "I am determined to finish my course."

FORGIVEN
SECURE
DISCIPLINED
PROSPEROUS
STRONG
TALENTED
MOTIVATED
PROSPEROUS
BLESSED
CONFIDENT

I am Strong:
YOU CAN
Handle It

CHAPTER FOURTEEN

Key Truth

You are full of "can do" power. You are strong
in the Lord. Your are more than a conqueror.
You have strength for all things through
Christ who empowers you.

THE
POWER
of "*I AM*"

The Scripture says, "The rain falls on the just and the unjust." Just because we're a person of faith doesn't exempt us from difficulties. We all go through challenges, disappointments, and unfair situations. It's easy to let these overwhelm us to where we think, *This is too much.* But God would not have allowed it if you couldn't handle it.

In difficult times, you have to talk to yourself the right way. Have a new perspective. You are not weak. You are full of "can do" power. You are strong in the Lord. The Apostle Paul put it this way: "I have strength for all things through Christ who empowers me." Listen to his declaration: "I am ready for anything. I am equal to anything through Him who infuses strength into me." He was stating, "The enemy may hit me with his best shot, but it won't stop me. I'm more than a conqueror."

The prophet Isaiah said, "Take hold of His strength." Every morning you need to do exactly that and declare, "I am ready for and equal to anything that comes my way. Almighty God has infused me with strength. He has equipped me, empowered me, anointed me, crowned me with favor, and called me to reign in life as a king." That's not just being positive. You're taking hold of strength. That's why the Scripture says, "Let the weak *say*, 'I am strong.'" When you say it, you're getting stronger. Shake off a victim mentality and have a victor mentality.

God is not going to deliver us from every difficulty. If He did, we would never grow. The Scripture says, "Our faith is tried in the fire of affliction." When you're in a tough time, that's an opportunity to show God what you're made of. Anybody can get negative, bitter, and blame God. But if you want to pass the test, you have to be a warrior.

Colossians 3 says, "God has given us the power to endure whatever comes our way with a good attitude." Dig your heels in and declare with Paul, "Nothing is a surprise to God. I can handle it. I'm ready for it. I'm equal to it. God is still on the throne. He is fighting my battles, and on the other side of this difficulty is a new level of my destiny."

The Apostle Paul said, "We know that all things work together for good to those who love God." Friend, God is in complete control. You don't have to get upset when things don't go your way. You have the power to remain calm. Quit letting little things steal your joy. Life is too short to live it negative, offended, bitter, and discouraged. Start believing that God is directing your steps. Believe that He is in control of your life. Believe that He has solutions to problems that you haven't even had. Stay calm and stay in faith; God promised that all things will work out for your good.

Greater is He that is in you than anything that comes against you. When you press past what's coming against you, on the other side of that difficulty is a new level of your destiny.

Consider This

What are you saying that is too much for you
to handle in your life? How will you take hold of God's
strength today and declare you can handle these matters?
What positive results do you expect to enjoy as you
tell yourself the truth that you can handle it?

....

....

....

....

....

....

....

....

....

....

....

....

....

....

....

....

....

....

....

What the Scriptures Say

"Fear not, for I am with you; be not dismayed,
for I am your God. I will strengthen you, yes, I will help you,
I will uphold you with My righteous right hand."

Isaiah 41:10

But those who wait on the Lord shall renew their strength;
they shall mount up with wings like eagles, they shall run
and not be weary, they shall walk and not faint.

Isaiah 40:31

Thoughts for Today

We are always in the forge, or on the anvil;
by trials God is shaping us for higher things.

Henry Ward Beecher

Storms make oaks take deeper roots.

George Herbert

Adversity causes some men to break;
others to break records.

William A. Ward

....
....
....
....
....
....
....
....
....
....
....
....
....
....
....

A Prayer for Today

Father God, thank You that I can take hold of
Your strength for whatever I am going through. Thank
You that I have "can do" power for all things through the
strength that Christ Jesus is infusing into me. Thank You
that You are directing my steps and making all things work
together for my good. I believe that You will help me to
press past whatever is coming against me and bring
me to a new level of my destiny.

takeaway
TRUTH

Get up every morning and remind yourself, "I'm ready for and equal to anything that comes my way. I am strong." If you will do this, God promises He will infuse strength into you. The Scripture calls it "can do" power. You will overcome every obstacle, defeat every enemy, and live the victorious life that belongs to you.

SECURE
DISCIPLINED
FORGIVEN
PROSPEROUS
ANNOINTED
MOTIVATED
TALENTED PROSPEROUS
STRONG
BLESSED

I am Anointed:
You Are
ANOINTED

CHAPTER FIFTEEN

Key Truth

God has placed His anointing on you.
The anointing is a divine empowerment that
enables you to do what you could not do on your
own, to accomplish dreams even though you
don't have the talent, and to overcome
obstacles that looked insurmountable.

THE POWER of "I AM"

We don't have to go through life doing everything on our own, trying to overcome challenges in our own strength, intellect, and hard work. We have an advantage. The Apostle John said, "You have an anointing from the Holy One." The anointing is a divine empowerment. It enables you to do what you could not do on your own. It will cause you to accomplish dreams even though you don't have the talent. It will help you overcome obstacles that look insurmountable.

In life's difficult times, you have to declare what Isaiah stated, "The anointing on my life is breaking every yoke." "The anointing is greater than this cancer." "The anointing is greater than this depression." "The anointing is causing me to overcome." Every time you say, "I am anointed," chains are broken. Fear has to leave. Depression has to go. Healing comes. Strength comes. Faith comes.

When David was a teenager, the prophet Samuel anointed him to be the next king of Israel, yet he spent years in the shepherd's fields after his anointing. The Scripture tells us to "reign in life as a king." You have a king's anointing, a queen's anointing, to live an abundant life, to accomplish your God-given dreams, to raise children who will be mighty in the land, to leave your mark on this generation. But on the way to your destiny there will be times of waiting where you have to be patient and keep doing the right things. You have to stay in faith and keep believing, *My time is coming. God has put the promise in my heart. I may not see how it can happen. But I have His anointing on my life.*

In the book of Judges, a woman named Deborah is described as "a mother in Israel." She didn't have an impressive position, title, influence, or prestige. She was a mom. Yet in a time of national crisis, Deborah knew God had put something on her that would cause her to excel. She took a step of faith that led to the liberation of her people.

How could this mother affect the whole nation? It was the anointing on her life. You are not limited by who you know, by how influential you are, or by how much income you have. There is something that supersedes talent, income, and experience. It's the anointing God has placed on your life. Quit making excuses as to what you can't do.

There will always be negative voices that try to talk you out of your dreams and convince you to settle where you are, but you have a king's anointing. You've been raised up. You have what it takes. You and God are a majority. If you will start taking steps of faith, doing what you can, God will do what you can't. He will bring the right people and open the right doors. He will give you the wisdom and the creativity. He will make it all come together. You're going to step into that king's anointing, that queen's anointing. Paul said it this way. "Don't get tired of doing what's right. In due season you will reap, if you don't give up."

Consider This

The anointing is only activated where there is faith. Write a declaration of faith for a fresh anointing on your life that brings help, favor, wisdom, and breaks every yoke that hinders you from stepping into the fullness of your destiny.

....
....
....
....
....
....
....
....
....
....
....
....
....
....
....
....
....
....
....
....
....

What the Scriptures Say

But you have an anointing from the Holy One,
and you know all things.

1 John 2:20

It shall come to pass in that day that his burden will be taken
away from your shoulder, and his yoke from your neck, and
the yoke will be destroyed because of the anointing oil.

Isaiah 10:27

Thoughts for Today

The Spirit-filled life is not a special, deluxe edition
of Christianity. It is part and parcel of the total
plan of God for His people.

A. W. Tozer

God wants to lead you to places you cannot get to without
Him, and He does that by the power of His Spirit. He can
bring you into the realm of the miraculous—not as a show, but
as a demonstration of His love and compassion for the lost,
hurting, or needy. Who among us doesn't want or need that?

Stormie Omartian

Will God ever ask you to do something you are not able to do?
The answer is yes—all the time! It must be that way, for God's
glory and kingdom. If we function according to our ability
alone, we get glory; if we function according to the power of
the Spirit within us, God gets the glory. He wants to reveal
Himself to a watching world.

Henry T. Blackaby

....
....
....
....
....
....
....
....

A Prayer for Today

Father in heaven, thank You that You have placed Your anointing on me to enable me to do what I cannot do on my own and to accomplish my dreams. Thank You that Your anointing breaks every yoke that would hold me back and helps me to overcome obstacles that seem insurmountable. Thank You that You have given me a royal anointing that I might reign in life as a king. I believe I am equipped and empowered to go where I've never been and do what I've never done.

takeaway
TRUTH

Every morning remind yourself, "I am anointed. I am equipped. I am empowered." Remember to always ask for that fresh anointing. You're going to go where you've never been. You're going to see negative situations turn around. Healing, promotion, and restoration are coming. You're going to step into the fullness of your destiny.

SECURE
DISCIPLINED
TRUST
FORGIVEN
PROSPEROUS
MOTIVATED
TALENTED PROSPEROUS
BLESSED
STRONG

I am Patient:
TRUST
God's Timing

CHAPTER SIXTEEN

Key Truth

God has established a set time to bring
His promises to pass in our lives, but He
doesn't tell us when they will be. You've prayed,
believed, and stood in faith. Now relax and enjoy
your life, knowing the answer has been set
in the future and is on the way.

THE
POWER
of "*I AM*"

In life we're always waiting for something—waiting for a dream to come to pass, waiting to meet the right person, waiting for a problem to turn around. When it's not happening as fast as we'd like, it's easy to get frustrated. But you have to realize that the moment you prayed, God established a set time to bring the promise to pass. Understanding that takes all the pressure off. You won't live worried, wondering when this is ever going to happen. You'll relax and enjoy your life, knowing that the promise has already been scheduled by the Creator of the universe.

Here's where it takes faith. God promises that there are set times in our future, but He doesn't tell us when they will be. The Scripture says, "Those who have believed enter into the rest of God." The way you know you're really believing is that you have a rest. You're at peace. You know the answer has been set in your future and is on the way.

There are set times in your future. You've prayed, believed, and stood in faith. Let me assure you that you're going to come into set times of favor, a set time where a problem suddenly turns around, a set time where you meet the right person, a set time where a good break thrusts you years ahead. That's what Habakkuk said. "The vision is for an appointed time. It may seem slow in coming, but wait patiently, for it will surely come." Not, "maybe come." Not, "I hope so." God has already set the date. The appointed time has already been put on your calendar. One translation says, "It won't be one second late."

A great prayer we should pray every day is, "God, give me the grace to accept Your timing." We live in a society that demands everything right now. We're being programmed for immediacy. But the Scripture says, "It's through faith and patience that we inherit the promises." God can see the big picture for our lives. He knows what's up ahead. He knows what we're going to need, who we're going to need, and when they need to show up. If what you are asking Him for hasn't happened yet, instead of being uptight, have a new approach. "God, You know what's best for me. I'm not going to live frustrated. God, I trust Your timing."

Your situation may be taking longer than you thought. Maybe it's something more difficult than you've ever experienced. So often we think we have to do it only in our own strength. This is when many people make quick decisions that end up only making matters worse. The Scripture says, "Be still and know that I am God." When you feel overwhelmed and you're tempted to take everything into your own hands, you have to make yourself be still. The battle is not yours. The battle is the Lord's. God is going to show His strength, His healing, His goodness, and His power like you've never seen before. Be still.

My challenge is, trust God's timing. Because you have faith and patience, God is going to give you the desires of your heart.

Consider This

Do you trust God enough to believe that your set times are coming? About what situation in your life is God saying, "Be still and know that I am God," right now?

....
....
....
....
....
....
....
....
....
....
....
....
....
....
....
....
....
....
....
....

What the Scriptures Say

For the vision is yet for an appointed time; but at the end it will speak, and it will not lie. Though it tarries, wait for it; because it will surely come, it will not tarry.

Habakkuk 2:3

Therefore do not cast away your confidence, which has great reward. For you have need of endurance, so that after you have done the will of God, you may receive the promise: "For yet a little while, and He who is coming will come and will not tarry."

Hebrews 10:35–37

Thoughts for Today

Most of the important things in the world have
been accomplished by people who have kept trying
when there seemed to be no hope at all.

Dale Carnegie

The faith of Christ offers no buttons to push for quick
service. The new order must wait the Lord's own time, and
that is too much for the man in a hurry. He just gives up
and becomes interested in something else.

A. W. Tozer

Nothing is ever wasted in the kingdom of God.
Not one tear, not all our pain, not the unanswered question
or the seemingly unanswered prayers. Nothing will be wasted
if we give our lives to God. And if we are willing to be patient
until the grace of God is made manifest, whether it takes
nine years or ninety, it will be worth the wait.

Author Unknown

A Prayer for Today

Father in heaven, thank You that You have established set times to bring Your promises to pass in my life. Thank You that You see the big picture for my life and You know what I'm going to need, who I'm going to need, and when they need to show up. Give me the grace to accept Your timing and rest in the fact that You've already scheduled things in for me. I believe that my times are in Your hands.

....
....
....
....
....
....
....
....
....
....
....
....
....
....
....
....
....

takeaway
TRUTH

Friend, there are set times in your future. Quit worrying about when it's going to happen. God can see the big picture. He knows what's best for you. Dare to say with David, "God, my times are in Your hands." You know God has it all figured out. Everything He has promised you will come to pass.

MOTIVATED SECURE DISCIPLINED PROSPEROUS CONFIDENT FORGIVEN MOTIVATED TALENTED PROSPEROUS BLESSED STRONG

I am Forgiven:
God LOVES
Imperfect People

CHAPTER SEVENTEEN

Key Truth

When we fall, God does not turn away from us
or love us less. Rather, He comes running after
us. His love is not based on our performance. It's
based on our relationship. We are His children,
and He loves us, imperfect as we are.

THE
POWER
of "I AM"

Most of the time we believe God loves us as long as we're making good decisions, resisting temptation, and treating people right. But the problem with this kind of reasoning is that we all make mistakes. No matter how good of a person we are, there will be times when we have doubts and fail. When we blow it, it's easy to think that God is far from us.

But when that happens, God loves you so much that He pursues you. He won't leave you alone until He sees you restored and back on the right course. He will express His love in a greater way. That's the mercy of God coming after you, saying, "You may have blown it and let Me down, but you're still My child. You may have lost faith in Me, but I haven't lost faith in you." Don't beat yourself up if you don't perform perfectly all the time. God loves imperfect people.

Think about Peter. Despite being warned by Jesus that he would deny Him three times, Peter did exactly that at the moment when Jesus needed him the most as a friend, when He was at His lowest moment. No wonder the Scripture says, "Peter went out and wept bitterly." Yet after Jesus rose from the dead, Peter is the first disciple whom the angel instructs Mary Magdalene to tell that Jesus is alive.

God is saying to Peter as well as to all of us who have fallen and made mistakes, "I'm not only alive, but I still love you. I still believe in you. If you will let go of the guilt and move forward, I will still get you to where you are supposed to be."

In the Scripture, it talks about "the God of Abraham, the God of Isaac, and the God of Jacob." Abraham and Isaac both seem to qualify, but Jacob was a cheater and deceiver who was known for making poor choices. What was God saying? "I'm the God of people who have failed, who have blown it, and who have had a rough past."

In the book of John, there was a lady who had been married five times. She was living with a sixth man. You could imagine the heartache and pain that she had gone through. And yet Jesus told His disciples He must travel out of His way to express His love for her. She is known as "The Woman at the Well." It's interesting that the first person Jesus revealed Himself to as the Messiah was not the religious leaders. It was a woman who had made so many mistakes.

Too often we get our performance mixed up with our identity. You may have failed, but you are not a failure. That's what you did. Failure is an event. That's not who you are. You are a child of the Most High God. You've been handpicked by the Creator of the universe. God is not judging you by your setbacks. Maybe you've blown a relationship, had an addiction, done something you're not proud of. Don't let that become your identity. You are free. You are clean. You are restored.

Consider This

If God pursued Peter after his utter failure, how about you?
Is there something in your life that you feel is beyond His
forgiveness? What is God saying to you about any
failure or mistake you have made?

....
....
....
....
....
....
....
....
....
....
....
....
....
....
....
....
....
....
....
....
....

What the Scriptures Say

If we confess our sins, He is faithful and just to forgive us our sins and to cleanse us from all unrighteousness.

1 John 1:9

"I, even I, am He who blots out your transgressions for My own sake; and I will not remember your sins."

Isaiah 43:25

....
....
....
....
....
....
....
....
....
....
....
....
....
....
....
....
....
....

Thoughts for Today

We tend to drag up our old sins, we tend to live
under a vague sense of guilt . . . we are not nearly as
vigorous in appropriating God's forgiveness as He is in
extending it. Consequently, instead of living in the sunshine
of God's forgiveness through Christ, we tend to live
under an overcast sky of guilt most of the time.

Jerry Bridges

Forgiveness transcends finite human reason.
The mere thought that one's entire sin account can be
utterly eradicated is staggering. . . . It speaks of guilt gone,
remorse removed, depression disappearing and emptiness of
life eradicated. What power there is in forgiveness! And it
all comes abundantly from the gracious hand of God.

Lewis Drummond

Why believe the devil instead of believing God?
Rise up and realize the truth about yourself—that all the
past has gone, and you are one with Christ, and all your sins
have been blotted out once and forever. O let us remember
that it is sin to doubt God's Word. It is sin to allow the past,
which God has dealt with, to rob us of our joy and our
usefulness in the present and in the future.

Martyn Lloyd-Jones

A Prayer for Today

Father, thank You that Your love and forgiveness
of me is not based on my performance but upon the
fact that I am Your child. Thank You that You love me,
imperfect as I am, and that every mistake I've made and
ever will make has already been paid in full by Jesus.
Thank You that when I fail You cleanse me and restore me.
I believe that You have set me free to become all
You have created me to be.

....
....
....
....
....
....
....
....
....
....
....
....
....
....
....
....
....
....

takeaway
TRUTH

Friend, your sins have already been forgiven in Jesus. Every mistake you've made and ever will make has already been paid in full. If you'll shake off the guilt and receive God's mercy, you will not only live freer but you will still become all you were created to be.

SECURE

CONFIDENT

FORGIVEN

PROSPEROUS

MOTIVATED

TALENTED PROSPEROUS

BLESSED

STE

I am Protected:
You've Been
FRAMED

CHAPTER EIGHTEEN

Key Truth

God has a frame around your times.
He has put a fence, a boundary, around your life.
Nothing can penetrate your frame that God doesn't
allow. Not only can nothing get in without God's
permission, but you can't get out.

THE POWER of "I AM"

When Scripture says, "The worlds were framed by the Word of God," it's not just talking about the physical *worlds*. The word in the original language is *eons*, meaning, "ages" or "times." It's saying that God has a frame around your times. He has put a fence, a boundary, around your life. Nothing can penetrate your frame that God doesn't allow. Trouble, sickness, accidents—they can't just randomly happen.

Not only can nothing get in without God's permission, but you can't get out. You can't make a mistake big enough to break out of that frame. It's a destiny frame. God won't let you get so far off course that you can't still fulfill your purpose. You may come right up to the edge, but you'll bump into the frame. God will push you right back.

In the Scripture, David experienced this frame. When a man named Nabal foolishly insulted David in public, David was so furious that he planned to kill Nabal and his men. But Nabal's wife convinced him to stop. She was a part of the frame. God ordained her to be there at the right time, to know exactly the right thing to say. Had David shed innocent blood, that mistake could have kept him from the throne. David went right up to the edge, but he bumped into his frame.

Jonah experienced the frame. God told him to go to the city of Nineveh, but he didn't want to, so he went in the opposite direction. You know the story. God will let you go your own way, but He is so merciful—at some point, you're going to bump into your frame. He let Jonah be thrown overboard, but He provided a fish as the frame. As with Jonah, you can run away, but the frame will always push you back toward your divine destiny.

In the Scripture, a man named Saul was the biggest enemy of the church. He hated believers. He was having them put in prison, doing more harm to God's people than any person of that time. One day he was on the road traveling to Damascus and a bright light shone down on him, blinding him. A voice said, "Saul, why do you persecute Me? Don't you know it's hard to kick against the pricks?" God was saying, "Saul, it's hard to keep kicking against the immovable frame. There is a calling on your life, a destiny for you to fulfill, and it's not to stop My work. It's to advance My work." Saul surrendered to God's way and became the Apostle Paul, who went on to write over half of the books of the New Testament.

Even death can't penetrate your frame. God has to allow it. The number of your days, He will fulfill. When a loved one dies, no matter what their age, we may not understand why they pass, but we can know that the enemy doesn't have the power to take them. God called them home and received them into His presence. When Jesus rose from the grave, He said, "You don't have to worry anymore. I hold the keys of death." He was saying, "Nobody determines your time except Me."

Consider This

In the light of God's frame around your life,
apply this powerful truth to whatever is worrying
and stressing you. Be specific.

....
....
....
....
....
....
....
....
....
....
....
....
....
....
....
....
....
....
....

What the Scriptures Say

So Satan answered the LORD and said, "Does Job
fear God for nothing? Have You not made a hedge around
him, around his household, and around all that he has
on every side? You have blessed the work of his hands,
and his possessions have increased in the land."

Job 1:9–10

But as for me, I trust in You, O LORD; I say, "You are my
God." My times are in Your hand; deliver me from the hand of
my enemies, and from those who persecute me.

Psalm 31:14–15

Thoughts for Today

A God wise enough to create me and the world
I live in is wise enough to watch out for me.

Philip Yancey

A providence is shaping our ends; a plan is developing
in our lives; a supreme and loving Being is making
all things work together for good.

F. B. Meyer

God is working behind the scenes to accomplish
His purpose. Nothing occurs in our lives by randomness
or chance. Seemingly small and insignificant decisions serve
His purpose for our lives. We think nothing of day-to-day
encounters, so-called accidents of history, but God uses
ordinary events to advance His purpose.

Dean Ulrich

A Prayer for Today

Father, thank You that You have put a frame around my life, a boundary that nothing can penetrate that You don't allow. Thank You that things don't just randomly happen to me and that You even have a way of keeping me from getting out of the frame. Thank You that You will fulfill the number of my days with divine protection. I believe that nothing can keep me from your destiny for my life.

....
....
....
....
....
....
....
....
....
....
....
....
....
....
....
....
....

takeaway
TRUTH

When you go through tough times, you have a bad break, you're facing a sickness, don't get discouraged. Remember, the frame is still up. There are boundaries around your life put in place by the most powerful force in the universe. Nothing will keep you from your God-given destiny.

SECURE
DISCIPLINED
FORGIVEN
PROSPEROUS
CONFIDENT
MOTIVATED
TALENTED PROSPEROUS
STRONG

I am Generous:
Become a
MIRACLE

CHAPTER NINETEEN

Key Truth

You are a miracle waiting to happen. God will bring people across our path so that we can be the answer to their prayer. You can lift the fallen, restore the broken, and be kind to a stranger. You can become someone's miracle.

THE
POWER
of "*I AM*"

Many people are praying for a miracle. They're asking God to send them comfort in a time of loss, help with their children, or to provide them training or work. We can become the miracle they need. God will bring people across our path so that we can be the answer to their prayer.

You are a miracle waiting to happen. Somebody you know is lonely and discouraged, saying, "God, send me somebody." You are that somebody. You can lift the fallen. You can restore the broken. You can be kind to a stranger. You can become someone's miracle.

We know that God can do miracles. But He's also put miracles in us. We can be the answer to someone's prayers, the good break they're looking for, the help they've been longing to have. It may be just teaching your coworker the skills you know. Or helping that family that's struggling with the rent. Or taking that young man to baseball practice with your son each week. It's no big deal to you, but it's a miracle to them. It's what will push them toward their destiny.

Perhaps you are the one who needs a miracle. Here's the key. If you will become a miracle, God will always make sure that you have the miracles you need. When you take time to invest seeds in others, the right people, the right opportunities, and the breaks you need will be in your future. God will get you to where you're supposed to be. That's what it says in Proverbs 11: "When you refresh others, you will be refreshed." If you want your dream to come to pass, help somebody else's dream come to pass. If you need a miracle, become a miracle.

Jesus told a parable in Luke 10 about a man who was attacked and beaten by bandits and left beside the road, almost dead. Both a priest and a Levite passed by and did nothing. Then a Samaritan man came by and became a miracle, carrying the man to a place of help and paying the costs. My question is: Which person are you?

When you get down low to lift somebody up, in God's eyes, you can't get any higher. The closest thing to the heart of God is helping hurting people. When you take time to restore the broken and wounded, encourage them, wipe away their tears, let them know that there are new beginnings—that's the religion Jesus talked about. And it provides opportunities for you to go to a higher level. Become the miracle.

We often don't realize we have the most powerful force in the universe on the inside. What may seem ordinary to us, no big deal, becomes extraordinary when God breathes on it. The Scripture says, "A gentle tongue brings healing." A phone call, giving someone a ride, taking them out to dinner, encouraging them in their dreams—there are miracles in you waiting to happen. Some people just need to know that you believe in them. When you tell them, "You're amazing. You're going to do great things," that may seem simple to you, but to the other person it can be the spark that brings them back to life.

Consider This

Someone you know has a need today that you can help with. Describe it, and list the steps you'll take to come alongside them with help.

....
....
....
....
....
....
....
....
....
....
....
....
....
....
....
....
....
....
....
....
....
....

What the Scriptures Say

Be kindly affectionate to one another with brotherly love,
in honor giving preference to one another; not lagging in
diligence, fervent in spirit, serving the Lord; . . . distributing
to the needs of the saints, given to hospitality.

Romans 12:10–11, 13

. . . through love serve one another.

Galatians 5:13

Thoughts for Today

It is not the possession of extraordinary gifts
that makes extraordinary usefulness, but the dedication
of what we have to the service of God.

F. W. Robertson

What an encouragement to realize that God has
reserved you and me for a special task in His great work.
In His hands we're not only useful, but priceless.

Joni Eareckson Tada

Too often we underestimate the power of a touch,
a smile, a kind word, a listening ear, an honest compliment,
or the smallest act of caring, all of which have the
potential to turn a life around.

Leo F. Buscaglia

....

....

....

....

....

....

....

....

....

....

....

....

A Prayer for Today

Father, thank You that You bring people across my path so that I may be the answer to their prayers and become their miracle. Thank You that I don't have be extraordinary or do extraordinary things to help people; I just have to be available and do what I can. Help me to encourage others to follow their dreams, to offer them my help, to speak a kind word, and to lift them up when they are hurting.
I believe that I am a miracle waiting to happen.

takeaway
TRUTH

Friend, you are the answer to somebody's prayer. You can give a rescuing hug or help a friend cross the finish line. You are the miracle that they're believing for. When you go out each day, have this attitude, I'm a miracle waiting to happen. If you will become a miracle, your light is going to break forth like the dawn. Your healing, your promotion, and your vindication will quickly come.

STAY**CONNECTED,**
BE**BLESSED.**

From thoughtful articles to powerful blogs,
podcasts and more, JoelOsteen.com is full of
inspirations that will give you encouragement and
confidence in your daily life.

AVAILABLE ON JOELOSTEEN.COM

 **today'sW○RD**

This daily devotional from Joel
and Victoria will help you grow
in your relationship with the Lord
and equip you to be everything
God intends you to be.

 **Joel Osteen
STREAMING**

Miss a broadcast? Watch Joel
Osteen on demand, and see
Joel LIVE on Sundays.

 **Joel Osteen
PODCAST**

The podcast is a great way
to listen to Joel where you
want, when you want.

CONNECT WITH US

PUT JOEL IN YOUR POCKET

Join our
community of
believers on your
favorite social
network.

 Get the inspiration and
encouragement of Joel Osteen
on your iPhone, iPad or Android
device! Our app puts Joel's
messages, devotions and more
at your fingertips.

 **JOEL**
OSTEEN
MINISTRIES

Thanks for helping us make a difference in
the lives of millions around the world.